P9-ARV-122

Put Beginning Readers on the Right Track with
ALL ABOARD READING™

The All Aboard Reading series is especially designed for beginning readers. Written by noted authors and illustrated in full color, these are books that children really *want* to read—books to excite their imagination, expand their interests, make them laugh, and support their feelings. With fiction and nonfiction stories that are high interest and curriculum-related, All Aboard Reading books offer something for every young reader. And with four different reading levels, the All Aboard Reading series lets you choose which books are most appropriate for your children and their growing abilities.

Picture Readers
Picture Readers have super-simple texts, with many nouns appearing as rebus pictures. At the end of each book are 24 flash cards—on one side is a rebus picture; on the other side is the written-out word.

Station Stop 1
Station Stop 1 books are best for children who have just begun to read. Simple words and big type make these early reading experiences more comfortable. Picture clues help children to figure out the words on the page. Lots of repetition throughout the text helps children to predict the next word or phrase—an essential step in developing word recognition.

Station Stop 2
Station Stop 2 books are written specifically for children who are reading with help. Short sentences make it easier for early readers to understand what they are reading. Simple plots and simple dialogue help children with reading comprehension.

Station Stop 3
Station Stop 3 books are perfect for children who are reading alone. With longer text and harder words, these books appeal to children who have mastered basic reading skills. More complex stories captivate children who are ready for more challenging books.

In addition to All Aboard Reading books, look for All Aboard Math Readers™ (fiction stories that teach math concepts children are learning in school); All Aboard Science Readers™ (nonfiction books that explore the most fascinating science topics in age-appropriate language); All Aboard Poetry Readers™ (funny, rhyming poems for readers of all levels); and All Aboard Mystery Readers™ (puzzling tales where children piece together evidence with the characters).

All Aboard for happy reading!

For my nephew, Henri. May you explore all of life's
amazing mysteries—J.B.

GROSSET & DUNLAP
Published by the Penguin Group
Penguin Group (USA) Inc., 375 Hudson Street, New York, New York 10014, USA
Penguin Group (Canada), 90 Eglinton Avenue East, Suite 700,
Toronto, Ontario M4P 2Y3, Canada
(a division of Pearson Penguin Canada Inc.)
Penguin Books Ltd., 80 Strand, London WC2R 0RL, England
Penguin Group Ireland, 25 St. Stephen's Green, Dublin 2, Ireland
(a division of Penguin Books Ltd.)
Penguin Group (Australia), 250 Camberwell Road, Camberwell, Victoria 3124, Australia
(a division of Pearson Australia Group Pty. Ltd.)
Penguin Books India Pvt. Ltd., 11 Community Centre, Panchsheel Park,
New Delhi—110 017, India
Penguin Group (NZ), 67 Apollo Drive, Rosedale, North Shore 0632, New Zealand
(a division of Pearson New Zealand Ltd.)
Penguin Books (South Africa) (Pty.) Ltd., 24 Sturdee Avenue,
Rosebank, Johannesburg 2196, South Africa

Penguin Books Ltd., Registered Offices:
80 Strand, London WC2R 0RL, England

Text copyright © 2010 by Jeff Belanger. Illustrations copyright © 2010 by Stephen Marchesi.
All rights reserved. Published by Grosset & Dunlap, a division of Penguin Young Readers
Group, 345 Hudson Street, New York, New York 10014. GROSSET & DUNLAP is a trademark
of Penguin Group (USA) Inc. Printed in the U.S.A.

Library of Congress Cataloging-in-Publication Data

Belanger, Jeff.
The mysteries of the Bermuda Triangle / by Jeff Belanger ; illustrated by Stephen Marchesi.
p. cm.
ISBN 978-0-448-45227-2 (pbk.)
1. Bermuda Triangle--Juvenile literature. 2. Shipwrecks--Bermuda Triangle--Juvenile
literature. I. Marchesi, Stephen, ill. II. Title.
G558.B45 2010
001.94--dc22
2009023678

ISBN 978-0-448-45227-2   10 9 8 7 6 5 4 3 2 1

THE MYSTERIES OF THE BERMUDA TRIANGLE

By Jeff Belanger
Illustrated by Stephen Marchesi

Grosset & Dunlap
An Imprint of Penguin Group (USA) Inc.

Welcome to the Bermuda Triangle

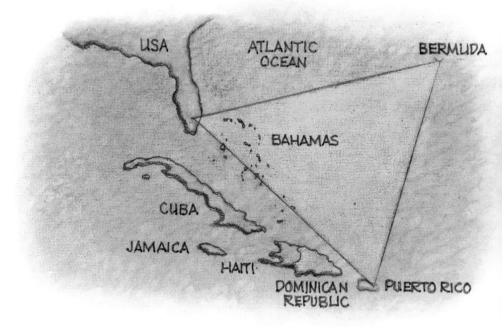

"This is Flight 19," called Lieutenant Charles Taylor over his radio. "My compass isn't working. I don't know where we are!" Lieutenant Taylor was returning to Fort Lauderdale, Florida, after a flight training mission near the Bahamas. He had been flying for hours, but couldn't find land. He thought he must be somewhere over the Atlantic Ocean . . .

but where? And why couldn't he find his way back?

Lieutenant Taylor was not the only pilot to get lost over the Atlantic Ocean. Over the past five hundred years, thousands of boats and airplanes have entered the region between Bermuda, Miami, and San Juan, Puerto Rico. But not all of them have come back. This section of cursed ocean is known as the Bermuda Triangle.

The Bermuda Triangle covers 440,000 square miles. That's a big area—and an even bigger mystery! What causes so many ships, planes, and people to lose their way here forever? Is bizarre weather at work? Perhaps there are strange magnetic forces? Maybe the travelers just had bad luck? Or maybe, just maybe, there is something even stranger going on here!

The Sargasso Sea

On August 3, 1492, Christopher Columbus set sail from Spain. He and his men were trying to find a new route to China and India. For weeks they sailed, not sure if they would ever see land again. This was during a time when people still believed the Earth was flat. As far as Columbus's men knew, they could head too far west and sail right off the edge of the world! The voyage made the men uneasy.

Finally a sailor called out. He saw something up ahead that looked like land! But as the ships sailed closer, they saw that it wasn't China. It wasn't even land! Instead, they were surrounded by brown seaweed. Columbus had found the Sargasso Sea, a floating mass of seaweed

in the middle of the Bermuda Triangle.
Columbus's men were worried that they
would get stuck in the seaweed. What
if it grew onto their ships and slowly
swallowed them, like a sea monster? Then,
to the crew's horror, the wind suddenly
stopped blowing. They *were* stuck!

For days the crew worried about being stuck in the Sargasso Sea too long. If they did not get out soon, they might not have enough food or water to make it back to Spain. But finally the wind began to blow again.

Soon Columbus's ships were free from the seaweed and sailing once more. But the Bermuda Triangle wasn't done with them yet. On the night of September 13, Columbus saw that the needle on his compass was not pointing north. This was

strange because a compass's needle *always* points north. Sailors count on this to find their way in the ocean. If a sailor knows which way north is, he can figure out what direction he is sailing. But Columbus could see by the stars that his compass was pointing in another direction! At night, sailors can steer their ships by the stars, but when the sun is out they rely on their compasses. How would the crew find their way during the day if they didn't know which direction to sail?

Luckily for Columbus, his compass corrected itself by the morning. But there was more strange behavior to come. On September 23, several large waves appeared in the calm sea. The water swelled a few times and then settled down again. Columbus had never seen anything like it before. What had caused this brief rush of water on an otherwise still day?

A voyage already filled with mystery was about to get stranger. On the evening of October 11, Columbus saw a strange light rising and falling in the distance. He

described the light like a flickering candle going up and down.

Land was spotted early the next morning. But Columbus's ship was still too far away to have been able to see light coming from the island. If the lights in the sky *had* come from the island, how had the islanders made them appear to Columbus from such a distance? Columbus could not explain it, but he would not be the last person to spot strange lights in the sky over the Bermuda Triangle.

The *Rosalie*

In 1840, a 222-ton French ship called the *Rosalie* was found drifting in the Sargasso Sea. The ship that spotted her pulled up close to see if help was needed. The men called out from their deck, but received no answer. The *Rosalie* looked empty, so a rowboat was sent over to investigate.

When the men pulled themselves onto the deck of the *Rosalie*, an eerie feeling came over them. Nothing looked out of place. Even the lifeboats were still in their proper positions. But where was the crew? Could pirates have raided the ship and taken them? The sailors went below decks. There was no sign of anyone down there, either—only a half-starved canary in its cage. All of the ship's valuables were still there, too! Nothing had been stolen. What kind of pirates would attack a ship and leave behind the valuables? But if it wasn't pirates, how had the crew left the ship without lifeboats? And why would they abandon their ship? To this day, no one knows. Sailors call vessels that have been abandoned like this ghost ships.

USS *Cyclops*

On February 16, 1918, the USS *Cyclops* set out from Rio de Janeiro, Brazil, for Baltimore, Maryland. The supply ship, which held 306 passengers and crew, planned to make one stop on the eastern coast of South America. The next stop was supposed to be Baltimore, a journey that should take about three weeks.

Eighteen days into their voyage, the *Cyclops* made an unexpected stop in Barbados to pick up additional supplies. The crew was confused by the stop. Why would they lose time on their trip when nothing was wrong? But they did as their captain ordered. Local officials could not explain the stopover, either. As best they knew, the *Cyclops* was not in need of anything.

On March 4, the *Cyclops* headed north toward Baltimore and into the Bermuda Triangle. The ship and the people on board were never heard from again. The United States Navy searched the ocean for the ship, but no sign of wreckage was ever found. The giant boat full of people had simply vanished!

Flight 19

Of all the strange occurrences and unexplained disappearances within the Bermuda Triangle, none are as famous as the case of Flight 19.

Just after 2:00 PM on December 5, 1945, flight instructor Lieutenant Charles Taylor climbed into his TBM Avenger. Taylor had two crewmen in his plane with him. He was leading four other airplanes with a total of fourteen men onboard in a

practice bombing run. The planes were to fly to the east near the Bahamas and drop bombs into the water. The men dropped their bombs on the practice targets. *Boom!* The bombs sent water high into the air.

With the first part of their job done, the crew continued flying northeast toward Grand Bahama Island. So far everything was going according to plan. After passing over the island, the planes were supposed to head north, then turn southwest and return home to Fort Lauderdale.

Somewhere along the way, Lieutenant Taylor realized that something was wrong. At around 3:45 PM, he radioed one of the other pilots in the group to say that his compass wasn't working and

that he didn't know where he was. Taylor was the leader, and it was his job to get the planes home safely. With their instructor confused, the other pilots also became uneasy. They were out over open ocean. If they ran out of fuel, would they survive?

Taylor's message to the other pilot was picked up by Lieutenant Robert Fox, who was flying south of Florida. Fox told Taylor to turn on his emergency radar equipment so that ground radar could find his plane and help guide him home. Fox even offered to try to find Taylor himself, but Taylor said that he didn't need help. He thought he knew where he was now. Taylor believed that he was over the Gulf of Mexico. If he just flew east, he was certain the group would see Florida. But the other pilots weren't so sure.

Before their compasses had stopped working, the planes had flown farther east and then north. The Gulf of Mexico was to the west of Fort Lauderdale. The men would have had to cross over Florida to get there. And yet, Taylor was certain that he was over the Gulf. It didn't make any sense, and the pilots were getting restless. To make matters worse, the sky had turned dark and cloudy. It was getting difficult to tell the difference between the sky and the ocean below.

The planes were fully fueled when they took off, but as the minutes ticked away,

so did their fuel. Some pilots in the group
suggested turning west to find land. The
other men agreed, and Taylor reported
that the planes were going to head west.
Soon after, he radioed to say that the
planes were going to turn and head east.

Why would Taylor change his mind
again? How could the experienced
pilot make such a mistake? There are
many islands to the east of Florida, but
somehow the planes couldn't find any
sign of land to help guide their way. They
were lost, and the situation was getting
dangerous.

With the minutes slipping away, the men were scared. There was no land in sight, and they were running out of fuel.

One control tower operator heard Taylor and the other pilots make a plan to land in the water when the first of their planes ran down to ten gallons of fuel. Taylor wanted to keep the group together because their best chance of survival and rescue would be to inflate their life rafts and wait for help. They would be easier to find if they landed as one large group rather than in many small groups.

Landing an airplane in the ocean is dangerous, but not impossible. If the Avengers had attempted the water landing, one or more of the crews should have been able to open the hatch and drop their self-inflating life raft into the water before their airplane sank. Some sign of the life raft or the plane would have been found by searchers. But they did not find anything. That means the planes must not have made the water landing they planned. Something else happened to them. But what?

Meanwhile, a search began for the planes. All of the boats and planes in the region were told about the five lost Avengers and asked to look out for them. Then, at 7:27 PM, a Mariner seaplane with thirteen men onboard set off to find the missing Avengers. The thirteen men on the Mariner were determined to rescue the crews lost somewhere in the Bermuda Triangle.

At 7:30 PM, the Mariner made a routine

radio transmission to its base. That was
the last time the Mariner was seen or
heard from again.

The following day, a massive search and
rescue mission was launched. Boats and
planes searched thousands of square miles
of ocean for floating debris or any sign
of the twenty-seven missing people. They
found nothing. No wreckage from the
Mariner or the five Avenger aircrafts was
ever recovered.

In 1991, a boat full of treasure hunters was using deep-sea cameras to search the bottom of the ocean off the coast of Florida. They were looking for shipwrecks that might contain sunken treasure. Imagine their surprise when their cameras picked up strange objects on the ocean floor. First a wing, then a tail fin. It was an airplane! They continued to search and found that it was actually five airplanes. When experts looked at the video tape, they realized

that the airplanes were Avengers. Had the planes of Flight 19 been sitting at the bottom of the ocean all this time? When the experts looked closely at the identification numbers painted on the wings of the planes, they knew they were not the same Avengers lost in 1945. They were actually planes that had separately crashed between 1942 and 1946. Flight 19 had not been found after all. Perhaps it never will be. It remains one of the Bermuda Triangle's greatest mysteries.

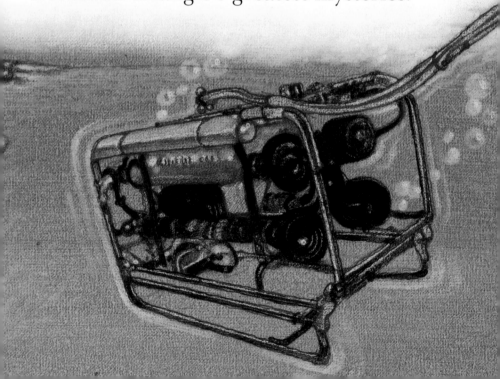

Flying through Electronic Fog

Since the pilots and crew of Flight 19 were never found, we have no way of knowing what really happened out there. But there are lots of people who have experienced unexplained activity within the Bermuda Triangle and survived to talk about it.

December 4, 1970, was a clear, sunny day, perfect for flying. At about 3 PM, Bruce Gernon took off in his small plane

from Andros Island in the Bahamas.
He was going to Miami, Florida. This
was a flight Gernon had made several
times before. He had planned an easy
route that would only take one hour and
fifteen minutes in clear weather. Gernon's
path would take him into the Bermuda
Triangle, but he didn't give the stories
about the area much thought. He had
passed through the Bermuda Triangle
before and never experienced anything
out of the ordinary.

Shortly after takeoff, Gernon noticed an oval-shaped cloud in the sky directly in front of his airplane. At first it seemed like a normal cloud. But it quickly grew in size. The cloud was about a mile away and nearly five hundred feet above the ocean. Gernon radioed Miami Flight Service and learned that the weather was clear. So he didn't worry too much about the cloud. He would just try to fly over it. He pulled back on his stick and the plane began to climb. As his plane rose, the cloud continued to grow. The cloud was almost yellow, not the bright white of normal clouds. Within seconds it surrounded the airplane. Gernon took his plane higher. Finally, at 11,500 feet, he broke through the top of the cloud and saw clear skies ahead.

Gernon looked back at the cloud. It was getting wider and starting to form a half circle, like a horseshoe behind his airplane.

Gernon looked ahead and saw another strange cloud in front of him. This cloud began on the surface of the ocean and extended upward for several miles. Gernon was an experienced pilot, but this was like nothing he had seen before.

Soon the two half-rings joined, forming a giant ring of clouds around his airplane.

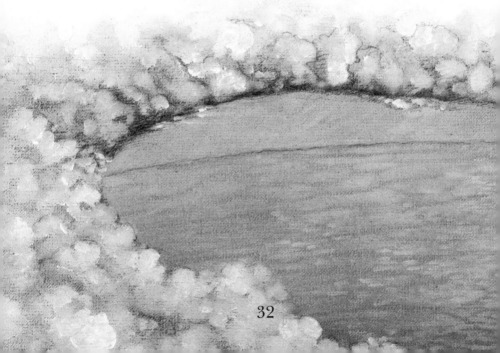

Gernon was flying in a thirty-mile-wide eye of clear air surrounded by clouds. When the ring closed, everything started to go wrong. Gernon's compass and other instruments stopped working. Something about this ring of clouds was affecting his airplane, and it was moving with him at over 150 miles per hour! Fortunately, Gernon could still hear the hum of his engine, which meant that he could still fly. But the situation was dangerous and Gernon was nervous.

Gernon decided to try to fly through
the ring of clouds. He pushed the plane
faster and entered the clouds. His small
aircraft bounced, and there were bright
flashes all around his plane. They were
not like lightning or anything else he
could identify, and there was no rain.
Whatever was happening, it wasn't good.

Gernon didn't want to risk the bursts of
energy striking his plane. He didn't want
to be in the center of the cloud ring, but
it seemed safer than flying *through* the
clouds. He slowed his plane down and
brought himself back into the clear air at
the center of the cloud ring. Suddenly, up
ahead, he saw a chance to break free.

Directly in front of him, Gernon saw clear, blue skies through a break in the clouds. Eager to get through, he sped up to 195 miles per hour and aimed for the blue sky in front of him. When he reached the edge of the clouds, a tunnel formed around his plane. The clouds began to tighten around him. He didn't know what would happen if he entered the dark, energy-filled clouds again. His only choice was to fly the plane as fast as it could go. As the tunnel closed in on him, he pushed his speed to 230 miles per hour! Such a high speed could be deadly if the engine overheated or failed, but he had to break free of the tunnel before it completely surrounded him. In only a few seconds, Gernon broke through the other side. He was free of the strange circle of clouds. But there was another problem ahead.

Gernon popped out of the tunnel and found himself in a hazy fog. Miami weather had reported clear skies, and there was no talk of storms or fog. So why was Gernon's airplane in a strange, soupy haze? Three minutes later, the skies around him turned to ribbons of fog. A few seconds later, the fog disappeared. Gernon was surrounded by blue skies, with no sign of the fog or cloud bank. Suddenly his instruments came back to life.

Miami radar informed Gernon that he was now flying over Miami Beach. The flight should have taken seventy-five minutes, but he had reached Miami in only forty-seven minutes! How could that be? According to Gernon, the tunnel he moved through must have moved him ahead in space and time. How else could he have reached Miami so far ahead of schedule? Gernon would later call this strange occurrence "electronic fog."

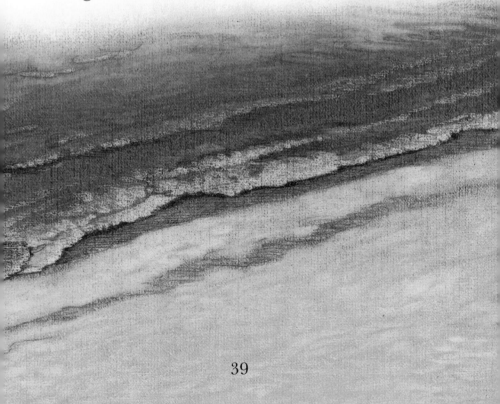

More Mysterious Fog

When there's only one report of a strange event, it's easy to believe that it didn't really happen. But Bruce Gernon wasn't the only person to fly through a strange fog in the Bermuda Triangle.

In June of 1986, Martin Caidin flew his plane from England to Florida. His path took him right through the Bermuda Triangle, but he wasn't worried. It was a beautiful day, with not a cloud in sight. Suddenly the sky filled with a milky fog. One minute Caidin could see for miles and the next he couldn't even see his plane's wings. The fog looked like a strange, yellow mud. Caidin checked his weather satellite. It said he was flying through clean air. The nearest clouds it saw were more than two hundred miles away!

Suddenly the instruments in Caidin's
plane stopped working. The compass
twirled around and around. The electronic
navigation gear, which would usually show
where the plane was, read "888888888."
Caidin tried to radio for help, but his
radio wasn't working, either. With no
instruments and no way to see where he
was going, he could end up way off course!

Up above, Caidin saw a faint blue patch of sky. Down below, he saw the ocean. He dipped the plane down toward the water to see if he could fly below the fog, but there was no change. He pulled back up to 8,000 feet and saw more of the same. Caidin was nervous, but he knew he had to stay calm if he was going to find his way out of the fog.

Caidin's best chance of getting out was to keep his plane pointed in the same direction as when he entered the fog. He tried to do this, but it was difficult to keep the plane on course when he couldn't see where he was going. When he was about an hour from Florida, the fog suddenly vanished! All of his instruments sprung back to life. He turned the plane around to get a look at the fog, but there was nothing there. Just endless blue sky. Had Caidin traveled through something similar to the "electronic fog" that Bruce Gernon had flown through sixteen years earlier? Martin Caidin was an experienced pilot, and even a flight instructor and investigator. But he had never seen anything like the fog before and could not explain it. It's just another mystery of the Bermuda Triangle.

Still Happening Today

On December 15, 2008, a twin-engine airplane carrying eleven passengers disappeared near the southern portion of the Bermuda Triangle.

The flight took off from the Dominican Republic and headed toward New York. The plane was supposed to stop on the Turks and Caicos Islands along the way, but it is unclear whether it actually did. Flight officials in the Dominican Republic said the plane left their island at about four in the afternoon and disappeared

from radar thirty-five minutes later
without arriving in Turks and Caicos.
United States Coast Guard officials said
the plane landed in Turks and Caicos and
vanished after taking off from the island.
But why were there two different stories?

The only thing officials know for sure
is that the airplane sent a distress call
shortly before it disappeared. But the
pilot did not explain what was wrong.
The Coast Guard searched the waters
around the islands but found nothing.
It seemed the Bermuda Triangle had
claimed another plane.

The Bermuda Triangle is one of the greatest mysteries of our planet. Some people believe there are strange magnetic forces coming from this area of the world that affect the ships and planes in the region. Others believe that large pockets of trapped gas, called methane, bubble up from the ocean and take down the boats and planes above. Or maybe the Bermuda Triangle is cursed, and it's just bad luck that has cost so many people their lives.

For now, this is one mystery that can't be solved. There is still too much we don't know about our oceans, our planet, and our universe. But the Bermuda Triangle forces us to keep asking the questions. And who knows. Maybe one day we'll find the answer!